THE BOOK OF
WIGGLES & TICKLES

G-4976

THE BOOK OF

WIGGLES & TICKLES

Wonderful songs and rhymes passed down from generation to generation

Compiled by John M. Feierabend

GIA FIRST STEPS • CHICAGO

Compiled by
John M. Feierabend

Artwork: Diana Appleton
Design: Nina Fox

GIA First Steps is an imprint of
GIA Publications, Inc.

ISBN: 1-57999-053-3
G-4976

Library of Congress Cataloging-in-Publication Data

The Book of Wiggles & Tickles: wonderful songs and rhymes passed down from generation to generation / compiled by John M. Feierabend.
     p. cm. – (*First Steps in Music*)
    Chiefly in English; includes several selections in German, one in Polish, and one in Scots, with English translation.
    Includes index.
    Summary: A collection of songs and rhymes that involve finger play, for infants and toddlers.
    ISBN 1-57999-053-3 (pkb.)
    1) Nursery rhymes. 2) Children's poetry. 3) Children's songs – Texts. [1. Nursery rhymes. 2. Songs. 3. Finger play.]
I) Title: Wiggles & Tickles. II) Title: Book of Wiggles and Tickles. III) Title: Wiggles and Tickles. IV) Feierabend, John Martin. V) Series.

PZ8.3 .B64458 1999
[E] – dc21
                                                           99-047435

During the past sixty years, families have been redefined. Where once there were large families living in close proximity, now the nuclear family is much smaller and more geographically dispersed. This shift in family community has strained the continuation of aural traditions. The playful songs and rhymes that were once shared by many generations of children, and adults with children, are gradually being forgotten. Those songs and rhymes that have demonstrated community affection and endorsement through the evidence of oral transmission are being replaced by commercially imposed ear candy, literature that provides a temporary rush but lacks long-term nutritional value.

The *First Steps in Music* series is an attempt to preserve the rich repertoire of traditional and folk literature; to enable today's families to recall and learn songs and rhymes that have nurtured wonder and joy in young people for generations. The authentic affection, innocence and wonder of these songs and rhymes have the potential to plant the seeds for sensitivity and imagination.

The songs and rhymes contained in this book have been gathered over the past twenty years. Many of the most interesting examples were collected from the elderly who often recalled songs and/or rhymes with great affection reminding them of loving moments they had shared with young people in the past.

Once there were many rhymes that evoked make-believe situations while wiggling baby's fingers or toes. Unfortunately, few are recalled today. Other rhymes which involved drawing a circle in baby's palm or on baby's tummy and then ending with a gentle tickle are also becoming extinct. Here, in one book, is the largest known collection of those songs and rhymes and their variations.

It is my hope that the collections of songs and rhymes presented in this series will help facilitate others in nurturing wonder in the lives of future generations.

John M. Feierabend

How to Wiggle

For many years baby's fingers and toes have played the roles of pigs, cows and many other characters. These playful rhymes continue to provide adults with a natural way to interact with their infants and toddlers in a mood of hushed wonder.

wiggle the fingers

wiggle the toes

have the child wiggle

When sharing these rhymes, wiggle baby's fingers or toes with the beat of the rhyme.

in most rhymes, unless indicated otherwise, start with the thumb or big toe and, with each character, work your way to the little finger or toe

Since young infants often prefer to keep their hands clenched, perform the wiggles on their toes. As they grow and become familiar with the rhymes, have them wiggle their own fingers or toes, wiggle the fingers or toes of a favorite stuffed animal or have them wiggle your fingers or toes while you recite the rhyme.

WIGGLES

Baby's Thumb

Baby's Thumb is Mister Gum.

wiggle each finger as it is named

Next comes Peter Point.
Lilly Long, Mrs. Ring,
And Pinky-Little One.
Down goes Peter Point,

fold each finger down as they are named

And silly Lilly Long.
Down goes Mrs. Ring,
And Pinky-Little One,
And around goes Mister Gum.

hold baby's thumb and make a circling motion

Das Ist Der Daumen (This Is the Thumb)

German

Das ist der daumen.
Der schüttelt die Pflaumen,
Der hebt sie alle auf.
Der trägt sie nach Haus
Und der Kleine isst sie alle auf.

Translation:

This is the thumb.
Shake the tree and down the plums
  come.
Gather the plums.
Bring the plums home
And the little one eats them.

Master Thumb

Master Thumb is first to come,
Then Pointer, steady and strong.
Then Tall Man high, and just nearby,
The Feeble Man does linger.
And last of all,
So neat and small,
Comes little Pinky Finger.

Little Tommy Thumb

This is little Tommy Thumb,
Round and smooth as any plum.
This is busy Peter Pointer,
Surely he's a double jointer.
This is mighty Tody Tall,
He's the biggest one of all.
This is dainty Reuben Ring,
He's too fine for anything.
And this little wee one maybe,
Is the pretty finger baby.

Variation

Here is Mister Thomas Thumb,
Round and fat as any plum.
Here is Mister Peter Pointer,
Surely he's a double jointer.
Here is Mister Toby Hall,
He's the biggest one of all.
Here is Mistress Finger Ring,
She's as fine as anything.
And here maybe,
Is the little finger baby.

Tom Thumbkin

Tom Thumbkin,
Willie Wilkin,
Long Daniel,
Betty Bodkin,
And Little Dick.

Variation 1

Harry Whistle,
Tommy Thistle,
Harry Whibble,
Tommy Thibble
And little Oker-bell.

Variation 2

Tom Thumblebum,
Johnny Goggins-Go,
Great Long Aunt Saireo,
Dumpty Deedum,
Peelewee Wee!

Variation 3

Tommy Tibule,
Harry Wibule,
Tommy Tissle,
Harry Whistle,
Little Wee-Wee-Wee.

Variation 4

Thumb He
Wizbee,
Long Man,
Cherry Tree,
Little Jack-a-dandy.

Variation 5

Thumbkin,
Pointer,
Middleman big,
Sillyman,
Weeman,
Rig-a-jig-jig.

with fingers running up baby's arm, giving a little tickle under baby's arm

Variation 6

Toe Tipe,
Penny Wipe,
Tommy Thistle,
Billy Whistle,
Tripping-go.

Variation 7

Thumb Bold,
Tibbity-Told,
Langman,
Lickpan,
And Mammy's wee,
wee man.

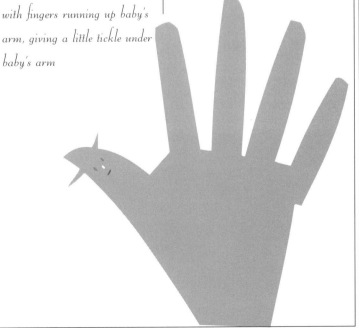

Thumbkin, Thumbkin Broke the Barn

Thumbkin, Thumbkin broke the
  barn.
Pinnikin, Pinnikin stole the corn.
Long backed Gray carried it away.
Old Mid-man sat and saw,
But Peesy-Weesy paid for all.

Variation 1

This is the man that broke the barn.
This is the man that stole the corn.
This is the man that stood looking.
This is the man that ran away.
This is the little woman who must
  pay everything.

Variation 2

This is the man that broke the barn.
This is the man that stealt the corn.
This is the man that ran away.
This is the man that telled it all.
And poor Pirlie-Winkie paid for all,
  paid for all.

Variation 3 (*Scottish*)

This is th' een wha' bruk the barn.
This is th' een wha' stul the corn.
This is th' een wha' telled it a'
An' this is the peeroe, weerie, minkie een
Wha' fell in burn wi' the hollow
  o'straw, and payed for a'.

This One...

This One Fell in the Water

This one fell in the water,
And this one helped him ashore,
And this one put him into bed,
And this one covered him o'er,
And then, in walks this noisy little
  chap,
And wakes him up once more.

This One Walked Out into the Wood

This one walked out into the wood
And caught a little hare,
And this one took and carried it
  home,
For he thought it dainty fare.
And this one came and cooked it up
With sauces rich and rare.
And this one laid the table out
And did the plates prepare.
And this little fellow the keeper told
What the others were doing there.

This One's Old

This one's old.
This one's young.
This one has no meat.
This one's gone to buy some hay,
And this one's gone to the village.

Row, Row, A-Fishing We'll Go

Row, row, a-fishing we'll go.

holding baby's hands push and pull them back and forth

How many fishes have you, Joe?
"One for my father,

wiggle each finger beginning with the thumb

One for my mother,
One for my sister,
One for my brother,
And one for the happy fisher boy,
Who eats his fish with yummy joy."

kiss baby's tummy

Said This Little Fairy

Said this little fairy, "I'm as thirsty as
  can be."
Said this little fairy, "I'm hungry, too,
  dear me!"
Said this little fairy, "Who'll tell us
  where to go?"
Said this little fairy, "I'm sure that I
  don't know."
Said this little fairy, "Let's brew some
  dewdrop tea."
So they sipped it and ate honey beneath
  the maple tree.

Let's Go to the Wood

"Let's go to the wood," says this little pig.
"What to do there?" says this little pig.
"To look for my mother," says this little pig.
"What to do with her?" says this little pig.
"Kiss her to death," says this little pig.

Variation 1

"Let's go to the wood," says this little pig.
"What to do there?" says this little pig.
"To look for my mother," says this little pig.
"What to do with her?" says this little pig.
"Fetch her home, fetch her home," says this little pig.

Variation 2

"Let's go to the wood," says this little pig.
"What will we do?" says that little pig.
"Look for my mother," says this little pig.
"What will we do?" says that little pig.
"Kiss her, kiss her, kiss her!" says this little pig.

Laughing Baby Susan

Laughing baby <u>Susan</u> knows,

substitute baby's name, wiggle all toes at the same time

How to wiggle all her toes.
Toes she jiggles while she giggles,
As she wiggles all her toes.

Seesaw, Margery Daw

Seesaw, Margery Daw,

wiggle one toe per line beginning with the big toe

The old hen flew over the malt house.
She counted her chickens one by one.
Still she missed the little white one.
And this is it, this is it, this is it.

The Dog Says, "Bow Wow"

The dog says, "Bow wow."
The cow says, "Moo, moo."
The lamb says, "Baa, baa."
The duck says, "Quack, quack."
And the kitty cat says, "Mee-OW."

gently squeeze the tip of baby's little finger as you say "OW"

Fire! Fire!

"Fire! Fire!" said Mrs. Dyer.
"Where? Where?" said Mrs. Dare.
"Up the town." said Mrs. Brown.
"Any damage?" said Mrs. Gamage.
"None at all." said Mrs. Hall.

Engine on the Track

Here is the engine on the track.
Here is the coal car just in back.
Here is the boxcar to carry the
   freight.
Here is the mailcar; Don't be late!
Way back here at the end of the
   train,
Rides the caboose through the sun
   and rain.

Hungry Piggy Snout

Here is hungry Piggy Snout;
He'd better stop eating or his tail will
  pop out.
Here is busy mother hen;
She likes to scratch for her chicken's
  ten.
Here is patient friendly cow;
She's eating hay from a big hay mow.
Here is Baa-baa, a woolly sheep;
Her wool keeps me warm while I'm
  asleep.
Here is fuzzy, fuzzy cat;
She likes to chase a mouse or rat.

run up baby's arm and give a little tickle

This Mooly Cow

This mooly cow switched her tail all
  day.
And this mooly cow ate the sweet
  meadow hay.
And this mooly cow in the water did
  wade.
And this mooly cow chewed her cud
  in the shade.
And this mooly cow said, "Moo, the
  sun's gone down,
It's time to take the milk to town."

I Have Five Pets

I have five pets that I'd like you to
  meet.
They all live down on Mulberry
  Street.
This is my chicken, the smallest of
  all.

start with the little finger and continue with
each finger

He always comes running whenever I
  call.
This is my duckling, he says, "Quack,
  quack, quack,"
As he shakes the water from his back.
Here is my rabbit, he runs from his pen.
Then I must put him back again.
This is my kitten, her coat is black
  and white,
She loves to sleep on my pillow at
  night.
Here is my puppy who has lots of fun,
He chases the others and makes them
  run.

run up the child's arm and give a little tickle

Mrs. Mason

Mrs. Mason broke a basin.
Mrs. Mack heard it crack.
Mrs. Frost asked, "How much it cost?"
Mrs. Brown said, "Half-a-crown."
Mrs. Flory said, "What a story."

Thicken Man

Thicken man, build the barn.
Thinner man, spool the yarn.
Longen man, stir the brew.
Gowden man, make a shoe,
Little man, all for you!

One Is a Lady

One is a lady
That sits in the sun.
Two is a baby
And three is a nun.
Four is a lilly
With innocent breast;
And five is a birdie
Asleep on her nest.

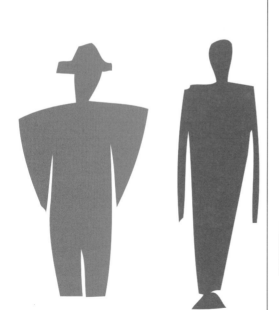

Das Ist Der Vater (This Is the Father)

German

Das ist der Vater lieb und gut.
Das ist die Mutter mit frohem mut.
Das ist der Bruder schlank und groß.
Das ist die Schwester mit dem Püppchen auf dem Schoß.
Das ist das Kindelein, das Kindelein klein.
Das soll die ganze Familie sein.

Translation:

This is the father short and stout.
This is the mother with children about.
This is the brother, tall you see.
This is the sister with doll on her knee.
This is the baby sure to grow,
And here is the family all in a row.

This Is the Mother

This is the mother,
This is the father,
This is the brother tall.
This is the sister,
This is the baby,
Oh, how we love them all.
hug baby and rock back and forth

Variation 1

This is the mother,
This is the father,
This is the brother, strong and tall;
And beside them stands the sister,
And the baby last of all.

Variation 2

This is the mother, good and dear.
This is the father, standing near.
This is the boy who plays with a ball.
This is the girl who plays with her doll.
This is the baby, the pet of all.
See the whole family, big and small.

Variation 3

This is the mother, kind and dear.
This is the father, sitting near.
This is the brother, strong and tall.
This is the sister who plays with her ball.
This is the baby, the littlest of all.
See my whole family, large and small.

This Little...

This Little Bear

This little bear has a soft fur suit.
This little bear acts very cute.
This little bear is bold and cross.
This little bear rests his head on the
  moss.
This little bear likes bacon and honey,
But he can't buy them;
He has no money.

Variation

This little bear has a fur suit.
This little bear acts very cute.
This little bear is bold and cross.
This little bear says, "You're not boss."
This little bear likes bacon and honey,
But he can't buy them;
He has no money.

This Little Bunny

This little bunny has two big eyes.
This little bunny is very wise.
This little bunny is soft as silk.
This little bunny is white as milk.
This little bunny nibbles away
At cabbage and carrots the live long
  day.

This Little Baby

This little baby rocked the cradle.
This little baby jumped in bed.
This little baby crawled on the carpet.
This little baby bumped his head.
This little baby played hide and seek.
Where's the little baby?

cover your eyes with both hands

Ooh, ooh, peek.

uncover eyes, then cover them again

Ooh, ooh, peek.

uncover eyes

This Little Chick

This little chick had corn today.
This little chick had only hay.
This little chick had worms, they say.
This little chick cried, "Peep, peep,
  peep,
Feed me or I'll weep, weep, weep."
This little chick had feather shoes.
He wore them out to get the news.

This Little Cow

This little cow eats grass.
This little cow eats hay.
This little cow drinks water.
This little cow runs away.
This little cow does nothing,
But just lies down all day.
We'll chase her, we'll chase her,
We'll chase her away.

with one finger, draw a circle in baby's palm

then run up baby's arm and gently tickle

Variation

This little cow eats grass.
This little cow eats hay.
This little cow looks over the hedge.
This little cow runs away.
And this big cow does nothing at all,
But lies in the fields all day.
We'll chase her and chase her
And chase her.

This Little Doggie

This little doggie ran away to play.
This little doggie said, "I'll go too
   some day."
This little doggie began to dig and dig.
This little doggie danced a funny jig.
This little doggie cried, "Ki! Yi! Ki! Yi!
   I wish I were big."

This Little Boy

This little boy found an egg.

   begin with little finger

This little boy cooked it.
This little boy peeled it.
This little boy salted it.
And this little fat boy ate it all.
And he was so thirsty he went for
   some water,

   walk your fingers up baby's arm

And he walked and he walked

   continue walking up baby's arm

And he drank and he drank.

   gently tickle under baby's arm

Variation

This one stole an egg.
This one fried it.
This one salted it.
This one ate it,
And this old dog went and tattled all
   about it!

This Little Mousie

This little mousie peeped with-in.
This little mousie walked right in.
This little mousie came to play.
This little mousie ran away.
This little mousie cried, "Dear me,
Dinner is done, it's time for tea!"

This Little Clown

This little clown is fat and gray.
This little clown does tricks all day.
This little clown is tall and strong.
This little clown sings a funny song.
This little clown is wee and small but
He can do anything at all.

Variation

This little clown is feeling sad.
This little clown is very mad.
This little clown is sleepy today.
This little clown is happy and gay.
This little clown is tiny and small,
He is afraid of everything tall.

This Kitty Said

This kitty said, "I smell a mouse."
This kitty said, "Let's hunt through
   the house."
This kitty said, "Let's go creepity
   creep."
This kitty said, "Is the mouse asleep?"
This kitty said, "Meow, meow,
I saw him go through the hole just
   now."

A Little Mouse

A little mouse came out to take a
   peek.
This one saw it.
This one ran after it.
This one caught it.
This one ate it,
Squeak, squeak, squeak!

'Round About

'Round about, 'round about,
   draw a circle in baby's palm
Here sits the hare,
In the corner of a cornfield
And that's there.
   tap the area between the thumb and index finger
This little dog found her.
   wiggle each finger starting with the thumb
This little dog ran her.
This little dog caught her.
This little dog ate her.
This little dog said,
"Give me a little bit, please."

This Little Tiger

This little tiger is very wild.
This little tiger is a loving child.
This little tiger has some big black
  spots.
This little tiger has small black dots.
This little tiger likes to prowl and
  smell,
But his teeth are too small to bite
  very well.

This Little Froggie

This little froggie broke his toe.
This little froggie cried, "Oh, oh, oh."
This little froggie laughed and was
  glad.
This little froggie cried and was sad.
But this little froggie did just as he
  should;
He hopped to the doctor as fast as he
  could.

This Little Kitty

This little kitty drinks her milk.
This little kitty's fur is like silk.
This little kitty wears soiled clothes.
This little kitty is Scratch Toes.
This little kitty can purr and sing;
Oh, she can do most anything.

This Little Puppy

This little puppy said, "Let's go out
  and play."
This little puppy said, "Let's run
  away."
This little puppy said, "Let's stay out
  'til dark."
This little puppy said, "Let's bark,
  bark, bark."
This little puppy said, "I think it
  would be fun,
To go straight home, so let's run, run,
  run."

This Little Squirrel

This little squirrel said, "Let's run and
  play."
This little squirrel said, "Let's hunt
  nuts today."
This little squirrel said, "Yes, nuts are
  good."
This little squirrel said, "They're our
  best food."
This little squirrel said, "Come climb
  this tree,
And crack these nuts; one, two,
  three."

This Little Elf

This little elf likes to hammer.
This little elf likes to saw.
This little elf likes to splash and
  paint.
This little elf likes to draw;
And this little elf likes best of all
To put the cry in the baby doll,
  "MAMA."

This Little Wind

This little wind blows silver rain.
This little wind drifts snow.
This little wind sings a whistled tune.
This little wind moans low;
And this little wind rocks baby birds,
Tenderly to and fro.

hug baby and rock back and forth

This Little Mountain

This little mountain finds the sun.
This little mountain drinks the rain.
This little mountain shades its eyes
And looks across the plain.
This little mountain is ready for bed
With a white cap on top of its head;
And this little mountain is up to its
  knees,
In the cunningest pointed Christmas
  trees.

the book of wiggles & tickles

Pigs, Pigs, and More Pigs!

The First Little Pig

The first little pig danced a merry,
  merry jig.
The second little pig ate candy.
The third little pig wore a blue and
  yellow wig.
The fourth little pig was a dandy.
The fifth little pig never grew to be
  big,
So they called him Tiny Little Andy.

A Fat Pig

A fat pig,
A short pig,
A long pig,
A thin pig
And a pig with a curly tail.

This Little Pig Makes an "Oink, Oink" Sound

This little pig makes an "oink, oink"
  sound.
This little pig is fat and round.
This little pig roots all around,
With his piggy snout he digs up the
  ground.
This little pig has a curly tail.
He eats his lunch from a shiny pail.
This little pig doesn't seem to care
If any of the other pigs get their share.

This Little Piggy Said

This little piggy said, "I want some
corn."
This little piggy said, "Where you
gonna get it?"
This little piggy said, "Out of Master's
barn."
This little piggy said, "You can't get
under the door sill."
This little piggy said, "Wee, wee, wee,"
All the way home.

Variation 1

This little piggy said, "I want some
corn."
This little piggy said, "Where you
gonna get it?"
This little piggy said, "Out of Papa's
barn."
This little piggy said, "I'm gonna tell
it."
This little piggy said, "Wee, wee, wee,"
All the way home.

Variation 2

This little piggy said, "I want some
corn."
This little piggy said, "Where you
gonna get it?"
This little piggy said, "Out of Papa's
barn."
This little piggy said, "I'll go and tell
it."

This little piggy said, "Queeky,
queeky,
I can't get over the barn door sill."

Variation 3

This pig got in the barn.
This ate all the corn.
This said he wasn't well.
This said he'd go and tell;
And this said, "Squeak! squeak!
squeak!
I can't get over the barn door sill."

Variation 4

This pig went to the barn.
This ate all the corn.
This said he would tell.
This said he wasn't well.
This went "Week, week, week,"
Over the door sill.

This Little Pig Had a Rub a Dub, Dub

This little pig had a rub a dub, dub.
This little pig had a scrub a scrub,
scrub.
This little pig-a-wig ran upstairs.
This little pig-a-wig called out "Bears."
Down came the jar with a great big
slam
And this little pig got all the jam.

This Little Piggy Went to Market

This little piggy went to market.
This little piggy stayed home.
This little piggy ate roast beef.
This little piggy had none.
This little piggy went "Wee, wee, wee,"
All the way home.

Variation 1

This little pig went to market.
This little pig stayed home.
This little pig ate roast beef.
This little pig had none.
This little pig went "Wee, wee, wee,
I can't find my way home."

Variation 2

This pig went to market.
That pig stayed home.
This pig ate roast meat.
That pig had none.
This little pig went to the barn door
And cried, "Week, week," for more.

Variation 3

This little pig went to market.
This little pig stayed home.
This little pig ate roast beef.
This little pig had none;
And this little pig said, "Wee, wee, wee,
Can't get over the barn door gate."

Wee Wiggie

with all of the rhymes on this page, begin by wiggling the littlest finger or toe, rather than the thumb,

and continue with each finger or toe

Wee Wiggie,
Poke Piggy,
John Whistle,
Tom Gristle
And old Gray Gobble,
  Gobble, Gobble.

Variation 1

Peedy-Weedy,
Polly-Ludy,
Lady-Whistle,
Lody-Wassle,
Great old Dommy died.

Variation 2

Acky Poo,
Penny Roo,
Rowee Whistle,
Merry Tossle,
Tom Bobble, Tom
  Bobble, Tom Bobble.

Variation 3

Ede Pede,
Pattie Odie,
Odie Whistle,
Miney Hossle,
Great big Gobble,
  Gobble, Gobble.

Variation 4

Little Wing,
Great Gin,
Long Bone,
Lick Pot,
Grumble, Grumble,
  Grumble, Grumble.

Variation 5

Little Pea,
Penny Roo,
Rhody Whistle,
Major Rossle,
Old Tom Bimble Bum.

Variation 6

Little Pig,
Pillimore,
Grimithistle,
Pennywhistle,
Great big Thumbo;
  Father of them all.

Variation 7

Itty Bitty Pid,
Piddy Iddie Ood,
Dodie Iddie Hissie,
Hissie Issie Aussie,
Great big old Hobble.

Variation 8

Little Pea,
Palley Lou,
Louty Whistle,
Maney Tausle,
And big..........Chooka,
  Chooka, Chooka.

How to Tickle

For years tickling songs and rhymes have continued to inspire a natural interaction between adult and child by presenting imaginary situations that create suspense and joyful resolutions in a playful manner.

on the palm   *up the arm*   *on the tummy*

these rhymes, unless indicated otherwise, begin with the adult
drawing a circle with one finger onto the palm of the child's hand

This action itself provides a gentle tickle and builds playful suspense for what will follow. Next the adult, accordingly, walks up the child's arm with one or two fingers "stepping" with the beat of the rhyme. For added suspense gradually slow down while walking up the child's arm. Finally, end by gently tickling the child under his/her arm.

With young infants, who prefer to keep their hands clenched, the adult can tap with one finger in a circle on the baby's tummy, keeping with the beat of the rhyme throughout.

TICKLES

Mousie, Mousie, Little Mouse...

PALM TICKLES

begin the following tickles by drawing a circle with one finger in baby's palm; then, with one or two fingers, walk up baby's arm; at the end of the rhyme, gently tickle under baby's arm

There Was a Little Mouse

There was a little mouse
And he lived right there;
And if anybody touched him,
He went right up there.

Variation

There was a wee mouse
And he had a wee house;
And he lived up there.
Then he went creepy-creepy,
  creepy-creepy
And he made a hole in there.

See the Little Mousie

See the little mousie
Creeping up the stair.
Looking for a warm nest,
There, oh, there!

The Little Mice Go Creeping

PALM TICKLE

The lit - tle mice go creep - ing,

creep - ing, creep - ing. The lit - tle mice go

creep - ing all through the house.

Verse 1

The little mice go creeping,

with one finger on each hand, walk up the baby from toes to head

Creeping, creeping.
The little mice go creeping
All through the house.

Verse 2

The big black cat goes stalking,

with entire hand, walk up the baby from toes to head

Stalking, stalking.
The big black cat goes stalking
All through the house.

Verse 3

The little mice go scampering,

quickly tickle baby from toes to head

Scampering, scampering.
The little mice go scampering
All through the house.

Creepy Mouse

Creepy mouse, creepy mouse,
All the way up to <u>baby's</u> house!

substitute baby's name

Variation 1

Creepy mouse, creepy mouse,
From the barn to the house,
Through the gully, gully, gully, gully!

Variation 2

Creepy mouse, creepy mouse,
All the way, all the way.
Creepy mouse, creepy mouse,
All the way home.

Variation 3

Creepy, crawly little mousie,
From the barn into the housie!

Variation 4

Here comes a mousey, mousey come,
Mousey come, mousey come;
And he gets you right there!

Variation 5

Creep, mousie creep.
Creep, mousie creep.
Looking for a little nest to go to
   sleep.
Here's one!

PALM TICKLES

Here Comes the Little Mouse

Here comes the little mouse,
Creeping, creeping through the
    house.
Over hill, over dale,
Tickle, tickle with his tail.

Creeping, Creeping, Creeping

Creeping, creeping, creeping,
Comes the little cat;
But bunny with his long ears
Hops like that!

'Round, 'Round, Around . . .

PALM TICKLES

'Round About

'Round about, 'round about
Ran a wee mouse.
Up a bit, up a bit
In a wee house.

Variation 1

'Rund aboot, 'rund aboot,
Went a wee moose.
Oop a bit, oop a bit
In a wee hoose.

Variation 2

'Round about, 'round about,
Gooseberry pie.
My father loves good ale
And so do I.

Variation 3

'Round about, 'round about
Apple pie.
Baby loves good ale
And so do I.

'Round About There

'Round about there,
Sat a little hare.
A cat came and chased him
Right up there.

Variation

'Round about there, sat a little hare.
The bow-wows came and chased him
Right up there!

'Round and 'Round the Cornfield

'Round and 'round the cornfield

draw a circle in baby's palm

Looking for a hare.
Where can we find one?

walk fingers up baby's arm

Right up there.

gently tug baby's hair

'Round and 'Round the Haystack

'Round and 'round the haystack
Went a little mouse.
One step, two steps
In his little house.

'Round and 'Round the Garden

'Round and 'round the garden
Like a Teddy Bear.
One step, two steps,
Tickle you under there!

Variation

'Round and 'round the garden

draw a circle in baby's palm

The little bunny goes.
Hippity hop, hippity hop,

walk up baby's arm

I'm gonna get your nose.

wiggle baby's nose

'Round About the Rosebush

'Round about the rosebush,
Three steps, four steps.
All the little boys and girls
Are sitting on the doorstep.

Round Ball, Round Ball

Round ball, round ball,

with one finger, draw a circle in baby's palm

Pull the chickies hair.
One slice, two slice,

with hand chopping motions, walk up baby's arm

Tickle 'em under there.

tickle under baby's arm

Variation

Round ballie, round ballie,
Pull the donkey's ear.
One slice, two slice,
Tickle them under here.

'Round and 'Round the Race Track

'Round and 'round the race track,
Get your tickets here.
One step, two steps,
Tickle under there!

PALM TICKLES

Shear the Sheep

Shear the sheep and trim the tree,
stroke baby's palm with your hand
But let the little lamb go free.
walk two fingers up baby's arm and give a little tickle

There Was a Little Hare

There was a little hare
And he ate the pasture bare;
And he crept and he crept,
Right up there.

Three Little Frogs

Three little frogs
Asleep in the sun.
We'll creep up and wake them,
Then we will run!

All Around the Worl'y

All around the worl'y
Chasing a little bear.
Right into a hole'y,
Right in there.

Washington Square

From here to there

with one finger, draw a circle in baby's hand

To Washington Square.
When I get there

with two fingers, walk up baby's arm

I'll pull your hair.

gently tug on baby's hair

Sullivan Square

From here to there

draw a circle in baby's palm

To Sullivan Square.
When I get there
I'll pull your ear.

with two fingers, walk up baby's arm and gently tug baby's ear

1, 2, 3

1, 2, 3,

with one finger, draw a circle in baby's palm

Father caught a flea.

pretend to pick a flea out of baby's palm

Put him in a teapot

close baby's hand

To drink a cup of tea.

bring baby's hand to your mouth and kiss it

Slowly, Slowly

Slowly, slowly, very slowly

with one finger, slowly draw a circle in baby's palm

Creeps the garden snail.
Slowly, slowly, very slowly

with one finger, walk up baby's arm

Up the wooden rail.

Quickly, quickly, very quickly

with one finger, quickly draw a circle in baby's palm

Runs the little mouse.
Quickly, quickly, very quickly

with one finger, walk up baby's arm

In his little house.

Roly Poly

Roly Poly
Shot a bear.
Where did he shoot him?
Right in there.

1.2.3

Oh Wie Langsam (Oh, How Slowly) *German*

Oh wie lang-sam, oh wie lang-sam kommt der schneck von
Oh, how slow-ly, oh, how slow-ly moves the snail from

sein-em fleck! Sie-ben lan-ge Ta-ge brauch-ter
place to place. Sev-en long days he needs un -

von dem eck sum an - dem eck.
til he finds an - oth - er space.

Potz, da wolt ich schnel-ler lauf-en, wenn ich so ein schneck-lein wär.
Potz, I'd sure-ly get there fast-er if I were a lit - tle snail.

Potz, da wolt ich schnel-ler lauf-en, wenn ich so ein schneck-lein wär.
Potz, I'd sure-ly get there fast-er if I were a lit - tle snail.

Verse

Oh, how slowly, oh, how slowly

with one finger, slowly trace a circle in baby's

palm

Moves the snail from place to place.
Seven long days he needs
Until he finds another space.

Potz, I'd surely get there faster

quickly trace a circle in baby's palm

If I were a little snail.
Potz, I'd surely get there faster

with two fingers, run up baby's arm

If I were a little snail.

gently tickle baby

What Do I See?

with one finger, draw a circle on baby's knee;
at the end, tickle baby's knee

What do I see? Baby's knee.
Tickly, tickly, tic, tac, tee.
One for a penny, two for a pound,
Tickly, tickly, 'round and 'round.

Variation 1

An old maid, an old maid
You will surely be,
If you laugh or if you smile
While I tickle 'round your knee.

Variation 2

If you are a gentleman
As I suppose you be,
You'll neither laugh nor smile
At the tickling of your knee.

Variation 3

Can you keep a secret?
I don't suppose you can.
Don't laugh and don't cry
While I tickle in your hand.

Variation 4

Lady, lady, in the land,
Can you bear a tickly hand?
If you laugh or if you smile,
You cannot be a lady.

Variation 5

Tickly, wickly in your hand,
If you laugh you'll be a man.
If you smile you'll be a lady,
If you cry you'll be a baby.

Variation 6

(can also be done as a knee rhyme)
Can you keep a secret?
I don't believe you can!
You mustn't laugh, you mustn't cry,
But do the best you can.

The Bee Went to the Barn

PALM TICKLES

There was a bee
Lived under the barn.
He carried his music box
Under his arm.

Variation 1

Bumble bee, bumble bee
Came from the barn.
Sting little Johnny
Right under his arm.

Variation 2

The bumble bee went
Under the barn,
With a bag of beans
Right under his arm,
And then he went, "Bzzzzzzzzzzz!"

Variation 3

Bumble bee, bumble bee

with one finger, draw a circle on baby's palm

Came from the bin.
Sting little Johnny

with one finger, walk up baby's arm

Right under his chin.

tickle under baby's chin

TUMMY TICKLES

Variation 4

Here comes a big bumble bee out of
   the barn
With a bundle of sticks under his arm;
And as he comes, he blows his horn.
Bzzzzzzzzzzz!

Variation 5

Bumble bee was in the barn
Carrying dinner under his arm.
Bzzzzzzzzzzz!

Variation 6

Bumble bee came out of the barn,
Sack of honey on his arm.
Bzzzzzzzzzzz!

Variation 7

The bee went to the barn
With bagpipes under his arm
And said, "Bzzzzzzzzzzz!"

Variation 8

There once was a bumble bee under
   the barn,
A bag full of cinnamon under each arm,
And when he got there he went,
   "Bzzzzzzzzzzz!"

TUMMY TICKLES

with a finger, draw a circle on baby's tummy; at the end of rhyme, tickle baby's tummy

These Are Baby's Fingers

These are <u>baby's</u> fingers,
substitute baby's name
These are baby's toes.
This is baby's belly button,
'Round and 'round it goes.

My Father Was a Butcher

My father was a butcher,
My mother cuts the meat;
And I'm a little hot dog
That runs around the street.

Tommy Thumb Is Up

Tommy Thumb is up.
Tommy Thumb is down.
Tommy Thumb is dancing
All around the town.

Old Hawk Goes

Old hawk goes
'Round and 'round and
Gets a little chicky.

The Cows Are in the Meadow

The cows are in the meadow
Falling fast asleep.
Along comes a bumble bee;
They hop to their feet!

Koci, Koci *Polish*

with one finger, trace a circle around baby's tummy; while speaking the words at the end, run fingers up baby's chest to his/her chin and gently tickle under baby's chin; at the end of the song, speak: "tooti, tooti, tooti, tooti"

Ko - ci, ko - ci łap - ci, Po - jed - ziem do bab - ci.

Gdzie bab - cia mie - szka? Bab - cia mie - szka Tu - taj!

Verse

Koci, koci łapci,
Pojedziem do babci,
Gdzie babcia mieszka?
Babcia mieszka Tutaj!

General Translation:

Tickle, tickle fingers,
Going to see Grammy.
Where does Grammy live?
Grammy lives here!

I'm Gonna Bore a Hole

I'm gonna bore a hole

draw a circle on baby's tummy gradually

getting smaller and smaller

And I don't know where.
I think I'll bore a hole… right…
THERE!

tickle baby's tummy

Variation 1

Bore a little hole.
I don't know where.
I believe to my soul
I'll bore it right there.

Variation 2

Bore a hole,

with one finger, draw a circle on baby's tummy

Bore a hole,
Stick a pea!

gently tickle baby's tummy

Variation 3

(*This one is a palm tickle.*)
Bore a hole, bore a hole,

draw a circle in baby's palm

Riiiiiiiiiiiiight there!

slide finger up and tickle under baby's arm

Bird Fly Away, Away

Bird fly away, away
Around in the air;
And light right here!

A Little Flea Went Walking

A little flea went walking
To see what he could see.
And all that he could see
Was <u>baby's</u> little tummy.

substitute baby's name and tickle baby's tummy

Index